CONTENTS

page 3
Welcome

page 4
Condition of the Heart
Past, Present, and Future

page 22
Covenant Love

page 36
Discovering Oneness

WELCOME

Our hope is that this syllabus will bless you and spark your marriage to "Fan the flame of your heart." The Lord instructs us to keep our marriage covenant. Despite the high failure rate of marriages, the condition of our hearts plays a crucial role in maintaining this covenant. Through the Holy Spirit's power, we have the authority to uphold it. Our prayers are dedicated to your wholeness, healing, and prosperity in your marriages and families. I know the thoughts that I think toward you, says the Lord, thoughts of peace and not of evil, to give you a future and a hope." **- Joe & Stephanie**

John 10:10 (NKJV) – "The thief does not come except to steal, and to kill, and to destroy. I have come that they may have life, and that they may have it more abundantly."

Jeremiah 29:11 (NKJV) – "For I know the thoughts that I think toward you, says the Lord, thoughts of peace and not of evil, to give you a future and a hope."

Condition of the Heart
Past, Present, and Future

What is the condition of our hearts?

Do we have hard hearts or hearts of flesh?

Ezekiel 36:26-27 (NKJV) – "I will give you a new heart and put a new spirit within you; I will take the heart of stone out of your flesh and give you a heart of flesh. I will put My Spirit within you and cause you to walk in My statutes, and you will keep My judgments and do them."

David's Prayer

Psalm 51:10 (NKJV) – "Create in me a clean heart, O God, and renew a steadfast spirit within me."

God's Strength

Psalm 73:26 (NKJV) – "My flesh and my heart fail; But God is the strength of my heart and my portion forever."

God's Care for Our Hearts

Restoration of your heart is the beginning of your ability to stand against the schemes of the devil.

God longs to heal our hearts. He cares about everything that concerns us, our joys and our sorrows.

Psalm 56:8 (NKJV) – "You number my wanderings; Put my tears into Your bottle; Are they not in Your book?"

In Jewish and middle-eastern homes in ancient times tear bottles were protected and buried with the owner at the time of death. In recent history scientist and artists have observed that dried tear drops are much like snowflakes in that they are all unique.

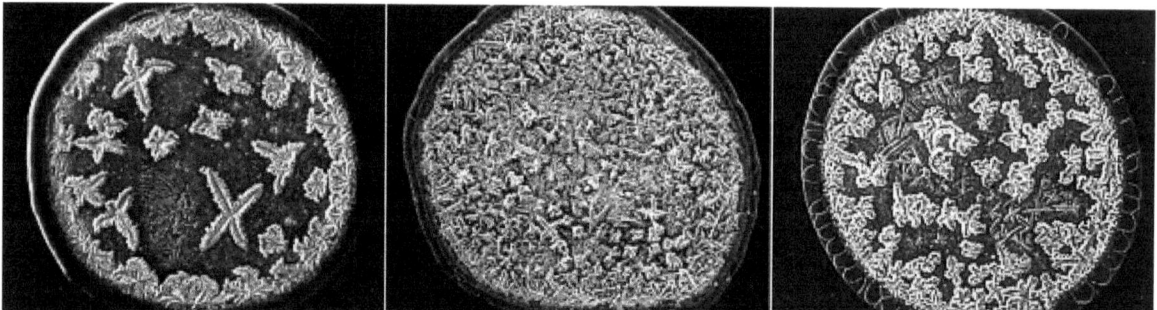

Images of dried teardrops under a microscope.   Credit: Photo: Maurice Mikkers

Notes

His   **Hers**

Condition of the Heart
Past, Present, and Future

Restoration of the heart comes through...

Redemption at the Cross

Ephesians 1:7-10 (NKJV) - In Him we have redemption through His blood, the forgiveness of sins, according to the riches of His grace.

Power of His Resurrection

Philippians 3:10 (NKJV) - That I may know Him and the power of His resurrection, and the fellowship of His sufferings, being conformed to His death.

Knowing and Believing God's Word

1 Thessalonians 5:23-24 (NKJV) - Now may the God of peace Himself sanctify you completely; and may your whole spirit, soul, and body be preserved blameless at the coming of our Lord Jesus Christ. He who calls you is faithful, who also will do it.

Walking in the fullness of who you are in the Word

Ephesians 3:19 (NKJV) - to know the love of Christ which passes knowledge; that you may be filled with all the fullness of God.

Repentance for Believing Lies

John 8:32 (NKJV) - And you shall know the truth, and the truth shall make you free.

1 John 1:5-7 (NKJV) - This is the message which we have heard from Him and declare to you, that God is light and in Him is no darkness at all. If we say that we have fellowship with Him, and walk in darkness, we lie and do not practice the truth. But if we walk in the light as He is in the light, we have fellowship with one another, and the blood of Jesus Christ His Son cleanses us from all sin.

Notes

His	Hers

Condition of the Heart
Past, Present, and Future

Widow's Plea

Believe God for everything He has for your marriage.

The Prophet's instruction shows the amazing love of God's provision.

2 Kings 4:1-7 (NKJV) - ¹ A certain woman of the wives of the sons of the prophets cried out to Elisha, saying, "Your servant my husband is dead, and you know that your servant feared the Lord. And the creditor is coming to take my two sons to be his slaves." ² So Elisha said to her, "What shall I do for you? Tell me, what do you have in the house?" And she said, "Your maidservant has nothing in the house but a jar of oil." ³ Then he said, "Go, borrow vessels from everywhere, from all your neighbors empty vessels; do not gather just a few. ⁴ And when you have come in, you shall shut the door behind you and your sons; then pour it into all those vessels, and set aside the full ones." ⁵ So she went from him and shut the door behind her and her sons, who brought the vessels to her; and she poured it out. ⁶ Now it came to pass, when the vessels were full, that she said to her son, "Bring me another vessel." And he said to her, "There is not another vessel." So the oil ceased. ⁷ Then she came and told the man of God. And he said, "Go, sell the oil and pay your debt; and you and your sons live on the rest."

The widow's story was not a public spectacle but a private encounter with the living God. Her request was survival. His answer was abundance. Don't limit what God wants to do for your marriage.

Jeremiah 33:6 - Behold, I will bring health and healing; I will heal them and reveal to them the abundance of peace and truth.

Notes

His **Hers**

Condition of the Heart
Past, Present, and Future

Heart of Forgiveness

In a marriage a husband and wife must have a heart of forgiveness.

Walk in it every day.

Matthew 6:14-15 (AMP) - ¹⁴ For if you forgive people their trespasses [their reckless and willful sins, leaving them, letting them go, and giving up resentment], your heavenly Father will also forgive you. ¹⁵ But if you do not forgive others their trespasses [their reckless and willful sins, leaving them, letting them go, and giving up resentment], neither will your Father forgive you your trespasses.

Matthew says we must first forgive for the Lord to forgive us. He paid the price; we must make a choice to walk in His fullness.

We cannot grow in what the Lord has for us with this behavior. Some reasons couples refuse to forgive are:

1. Repetitive actions (sin) by their spouses
2. Justification of their unforgiveness
3. Pride
4. Hurt is too overwhelming

All of the above makes our hearts vulnerable attacks of the enemy and hinders our ability to keep our heart soft to the Lord.

Notes

His | **Hers**

Condition of the Heart
Past, Present, and Future

Joseph's Example

The story of Joseph is in the book of Genesis. Joseph had many hardships that could have turned his heart to a rock only wanting vengeance and retribution. Instead he kept the Lord close. His brothers sold him into slavery because they were jealous of him. Joseph was purchased by Potiphar, the captain of the guard of the Pharaoh. Potiphar trusted Joseph with his entire household. Potiphar's wife attempted to seduce Joseph many times but Joseph's heart was right towards God. He hadn't allowed his heart to be hardened by what his brothers had done to him; therefore, he refused to fall into Potiphar's wife's trap and fled! Potiphar's wife lied and said Joseph tried to lie with her and he was thrown into prison. While in prison he was given charge of other prisoners by the jailer. Again he kept his heart right. "Because the Lord was with him everything he did prospered" Gen 39:22-23. Joseph eventually interpreted the Pharaohs dream correctly and was given favor by the Pharaoh and all of Egypt bowed before him. Because Joseph kept his heart right and favor was bestowed on him even to the point of complete restoration with his Father and brothers!

Gen 41:50-52 - [50] And to Joseph were born two sons before the years of famine came, whom Asenath, the daughter of Poti-Pherah priest of On, bore to him. [51] Joseph called the name of the firstborn Manasseh: "For God has made me forget all my toil and all my father's house." [52] And the name of the second he called Ephraim: "For God has caused me to be fruitful in the land of my affliction."

Gen 48:14 - But Israel stretched out his right hand and laid it on the head of Ephraim, who was the younger, and his left hand on Manasseh's head, crossing his hands, although Manasseh was the firstborn.

The birthright blessing was changed through Jacob blessing Ephraim first. Now we can be fruitful and then forget.

Forgiving Each Other

As we get the condition of our hearts aligned with the will of God, we can forget the past and allow God to prosper our relationship.

Matthew 5:23-24 (NKJV) - Therefore if you bring your gift to the altar, and there remember that your brother has something against you, [24] leave your gift there before the altar, and go your way. First be reconciled to your brother, and then come and offer your gift.

Forgiveness is so important to God that He wants you to forgive before He accepts your gift.

Notes

His   **Hers**

Condition of the Heart
Past, Present, and Future

Mark 11:25 (NKJV) - And whenever you stand praying, if you have anything against anyone, forgive him, that your Father in heaven may also forgive you your trespasses.

When people hold unforgiveness for others it affects not only them, but their marriage as well. A married couple is One Flesh.

Faith in Action
Forgive
Take time as a couple to ask each other for forgiveness. Put down all rights and weapons and be vulnerable. Help each other forgive and encourage one another.

Matthew 18:20-35 (AMP) - [20] For where two or three are gathered in My name [meeting together as My followers], I am there among them." [21] Then Peter came to Him and asked, "Lord, how many times will my brother sin against me and I forgive him and let it go? Up to seven times?" [22] Jesus answered him, "I say to you, not up to seven times, but seventy times seven. [23] "Therefore the kingdom of heaven is like a king who wished to settle accounts with his slaves. [24] When he began the accounting, one who owed him 10,000 [a]talents was brought to him. [25] But because he could not repay, his master ordered him to be sold, with his wife and his children and everything that he possessed, and payment to be made. [26] So the slave fell on his knees and begged him, saying, 'Have patience with me and I will repay you everything.' [27] And his master's heart was moved with compassion and he released him and forgave him [canceling] the debt. [28] But that same slave went out and found one of his fellow slaves who owed him [b]a hundred denarii; and he seized him and began choking him, saying, 'Pay what you owe!' [29] So his fellow slave fell on his knees and begged him earnestly, 'Have patience with me and I will repay you.' [30] But he was unwilling and he went and had him thrown in prison until he paid back the debt. [31] When his fellow slaves saw what had happened, they were deeply grieved and they went and reported to their master [with clarity and in detail] everything that had taken place. [32] Then his master called him and said to him, 'You wicked and contemptible slave, I forgave all that [great] debt of yours because you begged me. [33] Should you not have had mercy on your fellow slave [who owed you little by comparison], as I had mercy on you?' [34] And in wrath his master turned him over to the torturers (jailers) until he paid all that he owed. [35] My heavenly Father will also do the same to [every one of] you, if each of you does not forgive his brother from your heart."

Notes

His   **Hers**

Condition of the Heart
Past, Present, and Future

Luke 23:34 (NKJV) - Then Jesus said, "Father, forgive them, for they do not know what they do." And they divided His garments and cast lots.

Acts 7:59-60 (NKJV) - And they stoned Stephen as he was calling on God and saying, "Lord Jesus, receive my spirit." 60 Then he knelt down and cried out with a loud voice, "Lord, do not charge them with this sin." And when he had said this, he fell asleep.

Isaiah 43:25 (NKJV) - I, even I, am He who blots out your transgressions for My own sake; And I will not remember your sins.

A husband and wife should emulate Christ and the Church. We can walk in the forgiveness through the blood of Jesus.

How can a couple hold on to un-forgiveness in their marriage when they are "Bone of each other's bone and flesh of each other's flesh"? Jesus died on the cross for all our sins including adultery, abandonment and abuse.

Matthew 7:1-5 (NKJV) - Judge not, that you be not judged. 2 For with what judgment you judge, you will be judged; and with the measure you use, it will be measured back to you. 3 And why do you look at the speck in your brother's eye, but do not consider the plank in your own eye? 4 Or how can you say to your brother, 'Let me remove the speck from your eye'; and look, a plank is in your own eye? 5 Hypocrite! First remove the plank from your own eye, and then you will see clearly to remove the speck from your brother's eye.

Luke 6:37 (NKJV) - Judge not, and you shall not be judged. Condemn not, and you shall not be condemned. Forgive, and you will be forgiven.

Jesus showed us many years ago to look at people through His eyes. When you can do this you have much more compassion for your spouse and others.

Matthew 14:14 (NKJV) - And when Jesus went out He saw a great multitude; and He was moved with **compassion** for them, and healed their sick.

Notes

His **Hers**

Condition of the Heart
Past, Present, and Future

When we ask Jesus to allow us to see our spouses through His eyes we won't judge them, or anyone else for that matter.

When we judge others the same things we judge others about can fall upon us. Don't judge your spouse bless your spouse with the things God has for them.

Matthew 7:1 (NKJV) - Judge not, that you be not judged. When we walk in Forgiveness we can see our spouse the way God sees them we can agree with God's Vision for them.

Unresolved issues, un-forgiveness and resentment are all things that leave us hard hearted and unable to go on.

Faith in Action
Forgive
Ask the Lord to help you forgive and take these things to Him and leave them at the foot of the cross. "I will my will to be the will of the Father".

Hebrews 12:15 (NKJV) - looking carefully lest anyone fall short of the grace of God; lest any root of bitterness springing up cause trouble, and by this many become defiled;

Faith in Action
Bless One Another
Take time now to bless one another. Encourage one another in the areas you just dealt with. Break the cycle of unforgiveness in your lives with blessing!

Have you forgiven yourself? If you have not, forgive yourself now. If you don't forgive yourself shame will eventually overtake you. Ask the Lord to show you how He sees you. Don't let shame, guilt or pride rob you from victory.

Notes

His   **Hers**

Condition of the Heart
Past, Present, and Future

Shame

If you have come out of serious sin such as adultery or abuse, remember God still loves you. The devil wants to shame you. Shame is not from God.

2 Corinthians 10:12 (NKJV) - For we dare not class ourselves or compare ourselves with those who commend themselves. But they, measuring themselves by themselves, and comparing themselves among themselves, are not wise.

Faith in Action

Pray Together
Thank you, Jesus for healing the broken pieces of my heart. Fortify areas you have already healed and reveal any hidden place that needs your touch.

Notes

| His | Hers |

Covenant Love

Looking Back on the Beginning

Let's reflect on the beginning of our relationship.

- How did it happen?
- What do you remember?
- How different is it from what you imagined it would be?
- What did your parents think about your relationship?

Let's look at what it was like when you first met.

- Do you remember how you saw one another, when you first met?
- How did you feel when you spoke to each other?
- Remember those long phone conversations? How you tried to look your best when you were together?

Let's remember those days for a minute.

- Why did you marry one another?
- Do you remember looking into each other's eyes with excitement thinking about what your lives were going to be like together?

Most couples make plans about what their marriage will look like down the road.

What about the promises you made to each other? Not the ones at the altar, but the ones in private. Not the vows you made to be faithful, to love, honor and cherish, but other promises simpler promises.

Faith in Action

Reflect

Take some time to answer some of these questions and to remember and reflect on the beginning of your relationship.

Notes

His **Hers**

Covenant Love

Unequal Yoking

In the beginning of our relationships we all had hope. We all had dreams and expectations of what our lives were going to be together. Joe grew up in a religious home, but had no personal relationship with Jesus. Stephanie had gone to church since she was a baby. Stephanie accepted the Lord at nine years of age. Stephanie thought she could pray Joe into the Kingdom. Instead she was faced with an abusive man that eventually was unfaithful before and after the marriage. This ultimatly led Stephanie to fall away from the Lord and into adultry as well.

The word of God says not to be unequally yoked with a non-believer:

2 Corinthians 6:14 (NKJV) - Do not be unequally yoked together with unbelievers. For what fellowship has righteousness with lawlessness? And what communion has light with darkness?

Commitment and Mindset

Many have married for the wrong reason. Many have not asked God who they should marry. There was sexual sin in our relationship before marriage, which is a very common occurrence in this day and age. It set us up to fail. We had no respect or honor for each other. If this was your story. God forgives when we repent. Many of us had no idea what our commitment to each other actually was in the eyes of God.

- We were pretty sure we were committed to each other.
- We thought we would have love forever. Some of us go into our marriage with the mindset that any infedility automataclly means divorce.
- If he or she ever hits me we are done.

Disclaimer on Abuse

It is never ok to abuse anyone. It is a serious matter Missionaries2Marriages believes that abusive marriages can be healed. If you are in such a situation please seek help and safety. Gather others around you to pray for deliverance from the abuse not from the marriage.

Faith in Action

Pray Together

If you set yourself up with one of these types of vows you made. Pray against it right now in the name of Jesus! The devil may have just used those promises you made against you! - **God covers all of it!**

Notes

His

Hers

Covenant Love

Faith in Action
Forgive
Take time now to forgive each other for not fulfilling our parts of the dreams that did not come true and ask God for healing and new dreams.

Parental Blessing

What about blessing? Was your marriage blessed by your parents? How did your parents view your marriage? Did you feel blessed by your parents in your marriage?

Deuteronomy 30:19 (NKJV) - I call heaven and earth as witnesses today against you, that I have set before you life and death, blessing and cursing; therefore choose life, that both you and your descendants may live;

There is power in our words. A seed planted with our words will grow and multiply from its own kind! Good or bad. So if your parents did not bless your marriage you could be suffering the effects of that in your marriage.

You can break the curse over your marriage now. First forgive your parents. Now speak blessing over your marriage.

Faith in Action
Forgive
Take time now as a couple and forgive your parents. Pray a prayer of blessing over your parents.

Romans 8:37-39 (NKJV) - ^{37} Yet in all these things we are more than conquerors through Him who loved us. ^{38} For I am persuaded that neither death nor life, nor angels nor principalities nor powers, nor things present nor things to come, ^{39} nor height nor depth, nor any other created thing, shall be able to separate us from the love of God which is in Christ Jesus our Lord.

We again pray for our hearts to be softened to each other and the word of God.

Notes

His   **Hers**

Covenant Love

The Theory and Practice of Covenant

As we minister about Covenant we have realized that it is easy to tell people what Covenant is in theory. It is even easier to tell them to keep Covenant. But it is very difficult to keep Covenant if the condition of our heart is wounded.

Many times couples have had many incidents of wounding. The wounding has caused them to hardened their hearts towards each other and even God.

Many times the lack of love and intimacy in their marriage comes from the fact that they have divorced their spouse in their heart.

Malachi 2:14-16 (NKJV) - 14 "Yet you say, 'For what reason?' Because the Lord has been witness between you and the wife of your youth, with whom you have dealt treacherously; yet she is your companion and your wife by covenant. 15 But did He not make them one, having a remnant of the Spirit? And why one? He seeks godly offspring. Therefore take heed to your spirit, and let none deal treacherously with the wife of his youth. 16 For the Lord God of Israel says that He hates divorce, for it covers one's garment with violence," Says the Lord of hosts. "Therefore take heed to your spirit that you do not deal treacherously."

"Take heed to your spirit that you do not deal treacherously."

We clearly see in the above scripture that our marriage is a covenant by God's definition.

Many things happen over the course of a person's lifetime that causes the hardness of heart. Many times the heart slowly becomes hardened. Without notice, you just have had enough and stop being vulnerable in your heart!

Allow the Holy Spirit to have control over your mind, will, and emotions.

Definition:

Verb. 1. take heed - listen and pay attention; "Listen to your father"; "We must hear the expert before we make a decision" listen, hear. focus, pore, rivet, center, centre, concentrate - direct one's attention on something; "Please focus on your studies and not on your hobbies"

Notes

His   **Hers**

Covenant Love

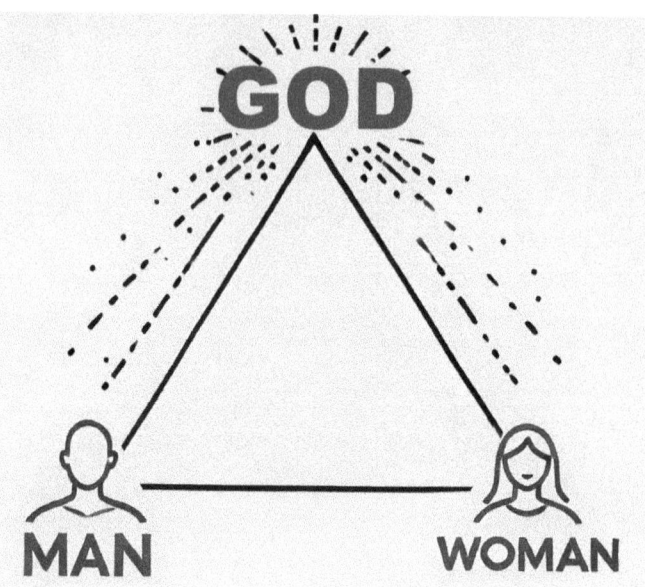

Covenant Diagram

Most Christians understand their marriage is a covenant. Some get the covenant confused with a legal agreement or contract which can be broken if one or both parties do not keep the agreement.

- Covenant is a supernatural commitment to the promises of God and to each other
- When we married we spoke vows that claimed we understood covenant.
- We made promises to one another that we would be "faithful until death" to our covenant.

Some people's vows have been put to the test of abuse, adultery and abandonment.

Many times these same people have searched for a true voice for help. Many times they have not been given the whole truth regarding their marriage covenant.

In every covenant God made with mankind throughout history; it required at least two participants.

We see that there are more than two in covenant. Many times as the going gets rough, we forget the third participant, God.

The promises we made to each other, man to woman and woman to man are important. However, without the third partner, God, in our marriage we fall short.

Notes

His

Hers

Covenant Love

God is this third benefactor. He happens to be the creator of marriage. He is the most important point in the triangle example of the Marriage Covenant. The promise is a supernatural lifelong ordinance.

Ecclesiastes 4:9-12 (NKJV) - ⁹ Two are better than one, Because they have a good reward for their labor. ¹⁰ For if they fall, one will lift up his companion. But woe to him who is alone when he falls, For he has no one to help him up. ¹¹ Again, if two lie down together, they will keep warm; But how can one be warm alone? ¹² Though one may be overpowered by another, two can withstand him. And a threefold cord is not quickly broken.

When we enter into a Marriage Covenant we are making a Blood Covenant.

- This is much like when we take communion. We are taking part of the body and blood of Jesus.

- All that is His we receive and all that is ours we give to Him. We do the same with our spouse. We give all of ourselves and receive all they have to give and vow "until death do us part".

- We give up all to be one. We give up our rights and our protection of ourselves to protect and be vulnerable to our spouse.

Notes

His | **Hers**

Covenant Love

Salt Covenant Ceremony to Have as a Couple

Salt was essential to life and had particular significance when it came to entering into agreements or binding arrangements. Salt covenants were used in ancient days as a way to publicly formalize and seal agreements and contracts. It was used to seal and finalize marriage agreements. In finalizing the marriage agreement, it was common that the two parties would individually bring their own salt in a container. They would then mix their salt with that of the other party into one new container as a way to show they are now joined together. After the common elements were mixed it was thereby understood that the only way for the marriage, or agreement, to be dissolved was for each granule of the individual parties to be returned to their original and separate containers. Short of that, the covenant could not be dissolved.

Biblical References to Salt Covenant

Leviticus 2:13 (NKJV) - "And every offering of your grain offering you shall season with salt; you shall not allow the salt of the covenant of your God to be lacking from your grain offering. With all your offerings you shall offer salt."

Numbers 18:19 (NKJV) - "All the heave offerings of the holy things, which the children of Israel offer to the Lord, I have given to you and your sons and daughters with you as an ordinance forever; it is a covenant of salt forever before the Lord with you and your descendants with you."

Mark 9:49-50 (NKJV) - "For everyone will be seasoned with fire, and every sacrifice will be seasoned with salt. Salt is good, but if the salt loses its flavor, how will you season it? Have salt in yourselves, and have peace with one another."

Notes

His | **Hers**

Discovering Oneness

The Importance of Prayer

Our prayer life as a couple is paramount to survival.

- Our prayer life brings us together in a deeper oneness in spirit, soul and body with each other and the Lord.
- Praying is the most important thing you can do to know the heart of God. Praying is solidifying your relationship with the Lord.
- We learn to hear the heart of our spouse. That's one reason why we pray.
- We are hearing God's heart together. We are agreeing with His heart in matters of our One-Flesh as well as other relationships.
- Prayer is the back bone of our growth in all areas.

Romans 8:26-29 (NKJV) - 26 Likewise the Spirit also helps in our weaknesses. For we do not know what we should pray for as we ought, but the Spirit Himself makes intercession for us with groaning's which cannot be uttered. 27 Now He who searches the hearts knows what the mind of the Spirit is, because He makes intercession for the saints according to the will of God. 28 And we know that all things work together for good to those who love God, to those who are the called according to His purpose. 29 For whom He foreknew, He also predestined to be conformed to the image of His Son, that He might be the firstborn among many brethren.

Prioritizing Prayer

Make the decision that daily prayer is a priority.

- **Releasing:** Through prayer together you as a couple release the power of the Lord into your one flesh, your family and your circumstance. God's Word comes alive when you pray to release His power.

- **Overcoming:** As a couple you can overcome any circumstance that comes against you. Together you stand and do not be moved until you receive victory.

- **Unity:** As you pray as a couple you will be in unity. You will have unity with each other and God. When you can stand unified as a couple you can move forward in all things. You build a hedge of protection around your Covenant and your family.

Notes

His   **Hers**

Discovering Oneness

Honoring Your Spouse

1 Peter 3:7 (NKJV) - Husbands, likewise, dwell with them with understanding, giving honor to the wife, as to the weaker vessel, and as being heirs together of the grace of life, that your prayers may not be hindered.

This scripture talks about "understanding". That is a huge aspect of Honoring. Everyone is different and we need to know the heart of our spouse. We need to have spiritual Intimacy, In-to-me-see. We are not referring to our sexual intimacy here. We are referring to seeing into each other's hearts.

- "Giving honor to the spouse as the weaker vessel" doesn't mean the man is superior in anyway. It means the man is the protector of the woman. We like to compare the wife to fine China. She is not weak but priceless!

- "Being heirs together of the grace of life" You have the privilege of growing old together with God's Grace covering you.

- "That your prayers may not be hindered." We all want our prayers unhindered so we need to follow the promises in 1 Peter 3:7

Understanding Submission and Love

In this section we will be going through Ephesians 5:22-33 verse by verse.

> **Ephesians 5:22-33 (NKJV) -** [22] Wives, submit to your own husbands, as to the Lord.

Many times wives take this scripture in a negative way, most likely because they have been wounded.

> **Ephesians 5:22-33 (NKJV) Cont. -** [23] For the husband is head of the wife, as also Christ is head of the church; and He is the Savior of the body. [24] Therefore, just as the church is subject to Christ, so let the wives be to their own husbands in everything.

The above scripture solidifies our previous comments. God is saying the husband is the head of the wife as Christ is the head of the church. Christ loves the church so much that He gave His life for the church.

> **Ephesians 5:22-33 (NKJV) Cont. -** [25] Husbands, love your wives, just as Christ also loved the church and gave Himself for her, [26] that He might sanctify and cleanse her with the washing of water by the word, [27] that He might present her to Himself a glorious church, not having spot or wrinkle or any such thing, but that she should be holy and without blemish.

Notes

His **Hers**

Discovering Oneness

Husbands are being instructed here to pour their lives out for their wives. Christ suffered and died for us that is what the Lord expects from us as husbands. We need to die to self in all things and put our wives first above all our needs, wants and desires.

> **Ephesians 5:22-33 (NKJV) Cont. -** [26] that He might sanctify and cleanse her with the washing of water by the word, [27] that He might present her to Himself a glorious church, not having spot or wrinkle or any such thing, but that she should be holy and without blemish.

The Lord is telling husbands that they are to be His hands to sanctify and nurture his wife with the Word of God. This is done through prayer, fasting and applying the Bible together to our marriage.

> **Ephesians 5:22-33 (NKJV) Cont. -** [28] So husbands ought to love their own wives as their own bodies; he who loves his wife loves himself. [29] For no one ever hated his own flesh, but nourishes and cherishes it, just as the Lord does the church. [30] For we are members of His body, of His flesh and of His bones. [31] "For this reason a man shall leave his father and mother and be joined to his wife, and the two shall become one flesh."

We know we are made One Flesh by the Lord. When scripture tells husbands they are to love their wives as they love their own flesh what is the word saying? Husbands are to nurture their spouse in all ways - Body, Soul and Spirit. Christ is our example. We are Flesh and Spirit with Him, so are we with our spouse. Because of this we leave our mothers and fathers and are joined. This also describes the relationship of Christ and the church.

Nurturing our spouse in prayer means we make it a priority. We also do spiritual warfare for them in our own prayer time. To nurture and nourish a body you feed it and give it exercise. To nurture our wives we must make sure we love God.

> **Ephesians 5:22-33 (NKJV) Cont. -** [32] This is a great mystery, but I speak concerning Christ and the church. [33] Nevertheless let each one of you in particular so love his own wife as himself, and let the wife see that she respects her husband.

So this is proof of how important your marriages are to God. It also explains why the devil spends so much time trying to destroy marriages. He wants to destroy the image of Christ on the earth, which is a Godly marriage.

Notes

His **Hers**

Discovering Oneness

Learning to Agree

Learning to come into agreement as a couple is essential.

- Praying for God's heart and His will for our decisions
- God cares about our smallest desires

Take time to really understand what your spouse is trying to communicate with you.

- Listen to each other
- Write your thoughts down to discuss them
- Pray for discernment
- Never try and solve a problem when you're in strife

Take communion together. It is an awesome time to remember what the Lord did for us at the cross in our prayer time together.

Job 1:10 (NKJV) - Have You not made a hedge around him, around his household, and around all that he has on every side? You have blessed the work of his hands, and his possessions have increased in the land.

Matthew 6:9-13 (AMP) - [9] Pray, therefore, like this: Our Father Who is in heaven, hallowed (kept holy) be Your name. [10] Your kingdom come, Your will be done on earth as it is in heaven. [11] Give us this day our daily bread. [12] And forgive us our debts, as we also have forgiven left, remitted, and let go of the debts, and have given up resentment against) our debtors. [13] And lead (bring) us not into temptation, but deliver us from the evil one. For Yours is the kingdom and the power and the glory forever. Amen.

Sexual Intimacy

We need to understand and believe how much God loves us. He desires intimacy with Him. We know we are One Flesh.

Genesis 2:23-24 (NKJV) - [23] And Adam said: "This is now bone of my bones and flesh of my flesh; She shall be called Woman, Because she was taken out of Man." [24] Therefore a man shall leave his father and mother and be joined to his wife, and they shall become one flesh.

Notes

His   **Hers**

Discovering Oneness

God supplied a whole book out of the Bible dedicated to covenant romantic married love. The Song of Solomon is that book. It has many metaphors and pictures of what marital intimacy is all about. The Song of Solomon is not only a basis for Covenant love between man and God. It is a description of man and wife in the marriage relationship. The Song of Solomon uses symbolic language as it talks about the Shulamite woman and her gardens. These examples are taken not only as the fruit of romantic love, but as blessings to the people of Israel.

Your daily prayer time with one another will build your sexual relationship

- Prayer is what allows in-to-me-see

- Knowing each other's heart comes from spiritual communication together with the Lord

- Learning God's heart together

- Prayer causes a deep connection with each other

- Your prayer time together as a couple will reignite your love for one another

- Pray for the intimate things of your hearts

- Pray for the Lord to entwine you together Body, Soul and Spirit

- Pray for God's protection over your intimacy

- Pray over the way you view each other

- Pray for purity and respect

Prayer is an absolute in intimacy. It is the most important thing we can do as a couple! Prayer together as a couple makes it possible to have true intimacy with each other and with the Lord. Our prayer time together increases our intimacy in body, soul and spirit. Our intimacy with the Father allows us to keep covenant by keeping our heart soft before Him. We can then hear His voice and know His will in all areas of our lives.

Notes

His

Hers

ABOUT JOE AND STEPHANIE

After years of physical abuse, adultery, and near divorce, Joe and Stephanie DeMott are healed and dedicated to empowering and mobilizing marriages around the world. While previously teamed with an international marriage organization for 29 years, they ministered to assemblies of thousands of couples as well as individual couples and home cell groups. In 2014, Joe and Stephanie launched Missionaries2Marriages.

The DeMott's have trained hundreds of couples to minister to marriages in the USA and other nations. Their testimony brings hope and encouragement to any marriage, and they minister to couples through teaching, the prophetic, and their own transparency. Joe and Stephanie have shared their story on the 700 Club as well as TBN's Praise the Lord show, and many other Christian television and radio programs. They are the authors of their testimony Booklet "Redemption" as well as a Marriage Course called "8 Keys to Breakthrough Victory in your Marriage.

Joe and Stephanie have been married since 1975 and have four grown children and grandchildren. Joe is a retired 30 year veteran Detective of the Denver Police Department where he worked in the Homicide Unit for eleven years. The DeMott's were called to marriage ministry in 1986 and have ministered in over 15 Nations in person.

SUPPORT MISSIONARIES 2 MARRIAGES

We are dedicated to ministering to marriages globally. Our "8 Keys to Breakthrough-Victory in Your Marriage" has reached couples across multiple nations, with translations in Italian, Spanish, Portuguese, and more. We're establishing Training Centers in several countries to further this mission.

You can make a difference:

Minister to Marriages
- Take what God has shown you about your marriage and pour into others

Support our work financially
- Assist in translations and travel
- Help establish Training Centers
- Join our short-term missions
- Sponsor our Online Breakthrough Meetings or TV outreach in Pakistan

Learn how to partner with us or donate.
Visit **www.missionaries2marriages.com**. All gifts are tax-deductible.

For more information, or to join our email list,
contact us at **info@missionaries2marriages.com**.
Together, we can bless marriages around the world.

PO BOX 7832
Broomfield, Colorado 80021
Office: 303-465-0342
Cell: 720-351-6211

www.ingramcontent.com/pod-product-compliance
Lightning Source LLC
Chambersburg PA
CBHW051400110526
44592CB00023B/2905